MY UROHS

My Urohs

Emelihter Kihleng

Kahuaomānoa Press
Honolulu, Hawai'i

~Kahuaomānoa Press~

President & Chief Editor	Brandy Nālani McDougall
Vice-President & Managing Editor	Ann Inoshita
Associate Editor & Treasurer	Ryan Oishi
Assistant Editors	Kai Gaspar
	Bryan Kamaoli Kuwada
	Jill Yamasawa
	Aiko Yamashiro
Faculty Advisor	Robert Sullivan
Typesetting & Book Design	Brent Fujinaka
Cover Design	Coleen Sterritt
	www.coleensterritt.com

Kahuaomānoa means, in 'ōlelo Hawai'i, "the fruit of Mānoa" and "foundation of Mānoa."

Kahuaomānoa Press is dedicated toward the publication and promotion of excellence in student art and literature. As such, every effort is made to privilege the student voice and perspective first and foremost.

Thank you to the editors of the following journals in which these poems first appeared:

"To Swim with Eels" in *Boundary 2,* Summer 2006

"Destiny Fulfilled?" in *Chain 12: FACTS,* 2005

"Micronesian Diaspora(s)" in *Xcp: Cross-Cultural Poetics 14,* 2004.

Kalahngan

Kalahngan Nohno, Pahpa, oh ahi peneinei kaoros. Kalahngan ong Wasahi oh Nahnep U, Nohno Emihko, Nohno Yoko, Sipwoli oh tohn Hideout, Deeleeann, Delga, Kadreen oh karohsie. Ma sohte kumwail e pahn sohte ahi urohs.

Kalahngan to those who have helped me most with my writing (and more): Juliana Spahr, Albert Wendt, Caroline Sinavaiana, Susan Schultz, Brandy Nālani McDougall and everyone involved with Kahuaomānoa. Kalahngan also to Cristina Bacchilega, Reina Whaitiri, the University of Hawai'i English Department and Center for Pacific Islands Studies. Kalahngan to my Aunt Tece for the beautiful cover, and to the writers whose words inspire me.

Contents

For you, Grandma,
my movie star

Patricia "Patsy" Ann Sterritt
July 5, 1932 – January 16, 2008

LIKIO

To Linda Rabon Torres[1]

How often do you shoot off your .22-caliber rifle?

Do you always shoot into your backyard jungle or do you sometimes shoot up in to the night sky? Perhaps aiming for a bird or a star?

I bet you are one of those people who fires off a couple of rounds every New Year after you've finished off a 6-pack of Bud

You would never admit to this now, but on the inside, did you secretly want to shoot someone, like one of those Chuukese neighbors of yours?

One of those Micronesians always causing trouble in your little "peaceful" Yigo neighborhood?

One of those stealers, pugua[2] chewers, heavy drinkers without any indoor plumbing?

What did you think was in your backyard jungle that April evening that made you pull out that rifle of yours?

Was it really those darn dogs always fighting and barking?

Did you hear the pig squeal?

---

[1] A woman from Yigo, Guam who fired her .22-caliber rifle into her backyard jungle to supposedly scare off wild pigs and dogs, killing a 14-year-old Chuukese boy, A.C. Kaselen on April 17, 2006. The case was initially dismissed, but she was re-indicted in September 2007, and pleaded guilty to charges of negligent homicide (*Pacific Daily News*, September 6, 2007). Kaselen's family believes that justice was slow because they are Chuukese (*PDN*, June 16, 2006).
[2] Chamorro word for betel nut.

The Love

I look at her in the car
sitting to my right
can she feel it?
as we drive
up and down the hills
of Yona
coming down past the Mini Camachile Store
approaching Route 4
we stare out at what looks more
incredible than the postcard
dark blue ocean
meeting light blue, almost white sky
I'm afraid she might feel it

ke saliel?[3]
how could you "forget" your new white tennis shoes?
we just bought them a few days ago at Payless
udahn ke pweipwei![4]
now what will you use?
you'll have to play tennis in your sohri[5]
you think we're so rich we can just go out and buy you a new one?

S
I
L
E
N
C
E

we buy you all these new clothes
new shoes
new sohri

---

[3] are you crazy?
[4] you're so dumb!
[5] from zori (Japanese); flip flops, slippers

4

new swimming goggles
and you "forget" your shoes?
you don't know how to take care of things

our favorite song comes on the radio
we sing:

we had so much fun
that we promised forever
and as time flew by
we got so much closer
saying goodbye became so much harder[6]

if she feels it too much
she'll want more

---

[6]Lyrics to "Fifty Plus One" by Xavier Pride, a popular song in Micronesia in 2006.

Destiny Fulfilled?

FACT: 1 box Maui Caramacs
            1 box Hawaiian Host Chocolate Covered Macadamia Nuts
            1 Hawai'i 2005 calendar
            1 Destiny's Child *Destiny Fulfilled* CD

mailed to my childhood friend in Tikrit, Iraq for Christmas

the chocolates intended to salivate her desert dry mouth
making her Army friends jealous
she has a friend in Honolulu and they only know people
in South Carolina and Tennessee

the calendar for her to mark off the days
28
27
26
palm trees
blue seas
green mountains
home

the CD a small distraction from falling bombs
i've thought about the hit song "Soldier" being on a CD
titled *Destiny Fulfilled*
wherein women are described as needing thug soldiers
to protect them
soldiers who "carry big things if you know what I mean"
my friend is a petite soldier

she is a citizen of the Federated States of Micronesia
"freely associated" with the United States of America
she could die for America
our friendly thug soldier
that continues to decrease its Compact Aid
to its "Coalition of the Willing" Island Nations

this thug soldier has already shot down
young Micronesian lives like hers
1 Palauan, 1 Pohnpeian, 1 Yapese, 2 Chamorros...[7]
with thousands more stationed across oceans
fighting for a foreign freedom

and meanwhile, the Marshallese,
Jimmy Mote, was just released
from Carver County Jail
wrongly imprisoned by Homeland Security
for trying to get a North Dakota State ID

the smiley thug soldiers keep recruiting
on Saipan, Majuro and Palau
brown islanders signing away their freedom
on islands seized by "liberation"
60 years before

I ponder these statistics as
she sends me email forwards
about "friends vs. best friends"
postcards that read
"On Patrol: Operation Iraqi Freedom"

is she the same woman
I met when we were 7?
neighbors in our small kousapw of Saladak
on the island of Pohnpei during those
carefree kool-aid, ice kehki, and mango days
we never heard of distant lands called Afghanistan and Iraq
our futures never given thought

---

[7] Since the initial publication of this poem in *Boundary 2* the total number of
Micronesian soldiers that have been killed fighting in the U.S. Armed Forces' "War
on Terror" has risen to 25. Ten "sons of Micronesia" died in 2007 alone (*Pacific
Daily News,* January 1, 2008).

POHNPEI OUTER SPACE

Nahn! I saw you on the MySpace
nomw space o songen lel![8]
I tried to IM you, but it wouldn't work
I requested you to be my friend
you have so many friends
100 plus! and all mehn Pohnpei
in GA, SC, Kansas City, Hilo, Honolulu...

my policy is that I'll accept you as my friend
as long as you're Pohnpeian
if you're not, then I have to know you personally
I don't want just anyone showing up on my profile
you know what I mean?

Nahn! why do all these Pohnpeians write like they're Black?
posting "holla back"
"I'm out"
"peace out"
when we all know they went straight from
Kolonia to Tennessee
never even met a real Black person in their life
don't even speak good lokaiahn wai[9]
after all, when they get to the States they only
hang around with other Pohnpeians
other Pohnpeians from the same part of Pohnpei too!

I'd rather have them write me in Pohnpeian
than in broken, fake Ebonics/English
i pahn kohwei pirapw mwangas nan sapwomwen[10]
is better than wassup homie, where you at?
Ohiei.

---

[8] Your space is so nice!
[9] English
[10] I'm gonna steal coconuts from your land

I know, I gotta work on my profile
it's so boring
I gotta add more pictures
pictures of me and my friends
holding Tequila shots
drinking straight from the pwotol en sakau[11]
eyes half closed from intoxication
so that I look popular, cool
but then if I make it too nice
with all the moving photo albums
and graphics
it'll look like I have no life
and spend all my time
pimping my space
and not doing my homework

---

[11] bottle of Pohnpeian sakau (kava)

Two Pohnpeian women talk about Eiht (AIDS)

lih laud (old woman):

Mehlel dir me Eiht Pohnpei?[12]
the first of her questions
when I got back
surprising
this coming from a sixty some year old Pohnpeian woman

serepein (girl):

I think lots of people have AIDS in Pohnpei now
they just haven't been tested

lih laud:

I sohte meir pwohng
I couldn't sleep last night
(in her Makiki apartment she shares with her daughters and their
    children)
there were these bugs (ticks) in the couch that kept biting me,
making me pwudong
I found blood in the cushions
and thought about Eiht
how the bugs could spread it
me and Ana (her daughter) threw the couch out this morning

serepein:

your apartment looks more spacious now
it's those politicians
those senators who brought AIDS to Pohnpei
all their traveling to the Pilipihn, Amerika for "conferences"
with prostitutes
then they come home and sleep with their wives and girlfriends

---

[12] Is it true that many people have AIDS in Pohnpei?

did you know Mihkel died of AIDS?
that's what everyone says
ke ese me e ohl mwauki ohl eh?
he slept with men

lih laud:

yes, aren't they the ones who started it?
the men who sleep with the men and
the women who sleep with the women
I don't know what it is that they do together

serepein:

ih sehse ma ih me tapiahda
(I don't know if that's what started it)
but I know that it's spreading
fast

lih laud:

it's also all the young people
going from one to the next
to the next

lih laud and serepein:

sengou[13] (they sing the word)

lih laud:

it's the men
grown men
irail me keiiu sengou

---

[13] promiscuous

I remember when my friend, Lucy
dragged me to watch the Eiht movie
she told me "ke anahne kilang"[14]
I told her I don't need to know about Eiht
I can't get it
but she forced me and I went
and I saw

---

[14] you must see

KOOL-AID[15]

doesn't taste good here in Honolulu
I wanna eat it sweating in the heat,
sitting on a rock,
under a guava tree
with my red-fingered friends
dip, dip our green mango
lick, lick our fingers
tongues turning dark red

---

[15] A mixture of ajinomoto (MSG), soy sauce, salt, and unsweetened kool-aid powder eaten throughout Micronesia.

KOREAN STORES

take a walk in my neighborhood
you'll see old men with missing teeth
young women with gold teeth
boys craving gum and lollipops going in and out
of *Makiki Food Center Liquor and Grocery*
we were frequent shoppers there
when my Nohno Lisa and Pahpa Sohs lived upstairs
the convenience of retail 30 feet away
creates needs for
Oceanic, Groove and 24 / 7 phone cards
cigarettes
Coke, Sprite, Strawberry Soda
SPAM, pwoaten kou[16] and Vienna Sausage
K and K Corner Mart
on the corner of Keʻeaumoku and Kīnaʻu
sells $5 pwuh[17]
$10 "fresh, frozen Pohnpeian sakau" from Molokaʻi
$1.25 yellow, red and purple combs
even urohs[18] and the kind of donuts sold back home
University Stop
I guarantee you every Micronesian in Honolulu proper
has been there at least once
many of us think of opening our own stores
catering to our own people
in the meantime, we keep giving the Koreans our
hard-earned money.

---

[16] literally, "can of cow"; corned beef
[17] betel nut
[18] Pohnpeian skirts, although in this case, the skirts are most likely from Chuuk

MICRONESIAN DIASPORA(S)

EK: *Ahmw tepin kohla Seipan oh dah ke wia? Ke doadoak?*

When you first went to Saipan what did you do? Did you work?

IR: *Ehng. Doadoak nan factory.*

Yes. I worked in a factory.

EK: *Hmm. Dah ke kin wia nan factory?*

What did you do in the factory?

IR: *Wil kopwe. Re kin dehkada likou irail kin kidohng kit, wilikada kilahng ekei, song ko, koakoadihla.*

Fold clothes. They sew the clothes and give them to us, fold them up and give them to others, like that, as it goes down.

EK: *Doadoak laud?*

Hard work?

IR: *Ehng. Apw seh reirei eh, kin kiden aramas apw ngehi ongieh udahn ih kin pwangadah, ih kin lok.*

Yes. But we were long, lots of people, but for me I really got tired, exhausted.

EK: *Awa depeh?*

How many hours?

IR: *Ih kin tep kulok isuh nek kulok isuh nisoutik.*

I start at seven and finish at seven in the evening.

EK: *Aoooo. Werei ieu.*

Wow. That's a long time.

IR: *Werei ieu mwoh. Pweh tepda nimenseng eh, kohditehieu kulok isuh nisoutik, nek, klous.*

That was a long time. Because we start in the morning and go all the way till seven in the evening till closing.

EK: *Ah ih kak idek rehmw ke kin ale tala depeh awa ehu?*

And can I ask how much you made in an hour?

IR: *Ehng. Komplihdla week riau oh, ih kin aleh talah silipwukih limeisek isuh.*

Yes. Completing two weeks, I get $357.00.

EK: *Aooo. Sohte itar.*

That's not enough.

Ah kumwail kin lunchbreak apeh?

Did you guys have lunch breaks?

IR: *Ehng. Eisek riau lunch, komoal lah oh kulok ehu tep, kohditehieu.*

Yes. 12:00 pm lunch, rest, and 1 o'clock start until finish.

EK: *Ah ko mehn ia kei?*

You and who else?

IR: *Mehn Pohnpei, mehn Ruk, mehn Kusaie, mehn Pilipihn.*

Pohnpeians, Chuukese, Kosraeans, Filipinos.

EK: *Wei eh, sohte mehn China iang?*

Oh really, and no Chinese?

IR: *Adkih mehn China me kin deidei eng kit.*

The Chinese sewed for us.

EK: *Oh.*

IR: *Aht kaun ko mehn Korea.*

Our bosses were Korean.

EK: *Wei eh. Ehri mehn China kau mihmi nan ehu pereh?*

Oh really. So the Chinese were in separate rooms?

IR: *Reh kin mwohd nan sehr irekdihdoh ehri kin deidei dohng kit ah se kin uhd wilik kilahng emen koakoadi.*

They sit in chairs in a line all the way down to us, and they sew, and give it to us, and we fold them and pass it down and onwards.

(she spits betelnut juice)

Reh kin dir nan ehu sehr oh kak meh siliakan samwah mie, pweh udahn kin reirei koadihla, apw kaidehn pil ehu te, ehu room oh udahn kin line mwein kak meh wenou, ah kohla nih ehu room kak pil line wenou de isuh wen dir.

They were so many on one chair, could have more than thirty because it is so long, all the way down, but not just one. One room would have a line of six to another room with six or seven, since so many.

II: DREAMERS

1

*Ih koalauh, ei doadoak oh, ong ie ih mwauki ei kin aleh nei sent, wiahki
nsenei song koh eh. Ah ei mihmi Pohnpei eh, ih sohte kin aleh songehn
lapalahn sentuwoh. Apw ih men pwurala likioh, apw ih sohte men kohla
ngehi pwurala Seipan.*

When I went, I worked, for me I liked it when I got my own money,
doing what I want with it. But staying in Pohnpei, I never get that
much money. But I want to go back out there, but I don't want to go
back to Saipan.

my dream is to bring my two babies with me
to Hawai'i, there are lots of us there and
I hear it's the nicest
get a job and eventually bring my parents
to live with us too

2

they are lucky these Micronesians
coming from their impoverished islands
I've been there, they have no sewage system
Filthy, nothing for them to do all day
yea, so they might have to work a few extra hours
I give them the American dream

3

North Pacific give me job at SeaWorld
Janitor, I don't like but cannot leave
they stop paying the rent
my wife and baby at home
they took the TV and the bed
we sleep on floor

4
yes, they are my people therefore
I know the economic conditions on our islands
the FSM government encourages migration
I'm doing them a favor

2
you can import maybe a thousand a year,
and you don't have to worry about a quota system.
they can fill any labor shortage you can find.

5
these islanders are taken advantage of
literally bought for $5,500
they become indentured servants held in
debt bondage upon arrival
with no ticket home
we are trying to do whatever we can

2
Micronesians don't need a lot to
keep entertained, they play
bingo and drink all night and
on their days off they sleep
they are happy, they don't complain

6
when we came, me and my sister
we only have our slipper on our feet
no clothes and when we got to the
apartment we cry and cry
they said it would be nice
and we know they lie

III: WHITE HOUSE

they broke my body on the inside.
I walk into the big white house.
already I smell it, Pohnpei hospital smell but worse.
pwohn kent, piss, stink.
piss and old people smell.
new smell to me.
I see them sitting, quiet some of them,
some talking to themself but not crazy, just alone.
I feel scared and the tile was sticky like white stuff from *pwomaria* tree.

my head hurt because I so sad for them.
so sorry for the old white people and some black.
so sad. I wonder where are their children?
they must be dead.
I never knew old people by themself, no son, no daughter.
in wheel chair, in bed, shake back and forth.
I want to cry for the children gone.

I don't understand.
I cannot.
back home no piss smell on them.
no shit smell.
only coconut oil smell. nice smell.

*Nohno Pahpa Nohno Pahpa Nohno Pahpa Nohno Pahpa Nohno Pahpa
Nohno Pahpa*

LIMPOAK MEHLEL!

only love we show to grandma, grandpa, uncle, auntie.
all of them our mom and dad, we love them all.
sweet smell.

AMERIKA.
in this rich country, I so surprise.

so much french fries and cheeseburger,
so much Safeway, WalMart, Mall, SUV,
big house with fence, nice yard with flower.
I think oh, must be so much happiness and so much love.
I don't understand.
why grandma and grandpa alone?
no one visit, no one bring happy meal, no one talk to them.
I talk to them, even in my language.
I know they don't understand.
I don't care.
they want to hear my voice.

I tell them:

mah ke mihmi sapweioh ke sohte pahn loleid,
ke sohte pahn kelekelepw.
seh pahn apwalihiuk. kamwengeiiuk.
kiht nomw seri limpoak.

I tell them:

if you from my island. you never be lonely. you never be alone. you
no scream late in the night time. no cry. no piss smell, never. I am
your child and I feed you. the children you feed and their baby too.

NAHNEP LOVES CARPET

she lies on the carpet
in every room
on her stomach
her large brown body
in her flower mwumwu
has become familiar like
a new piece of furniture
you've had for a month
except it laughs a lot and wiggles

her fragrance flows
through the concrete walls
she's at home
taking long baths in the tub
reading her pwuhk sarawi
with her big old lady glasses
gossiping about everyone in U
giggling about sex
eating lots of pilawa with peanut butter
whispering about body parts
singing about Jesus

she makes the 15th floor shake
as we revel in her presence

NAHNEP, ON SUNSETS

ohs! ihs me men kilang ketipino kihrla?[19]
she wasn't raised to think anything of sunsets
so the sun goes up
it must come down
who cares?
my mom and I, the mehn wai[20]
took her, the soupeidi[21]
down to Waikiki by the aquarium
we gazed at each other, the skyline
thinking, how strange not to be at Pohnpil
listening to the river, the dogs, the darkness
but instead watching, waiting for this foreign sunset.

---

[19] Who wants to watch the sun go down?
[20] Foreigners or white people
[21] high status person from a ruling clan; a chief, in this case a chiefly woman

SAPW SARAWI

E pwoh wih (it smells fatty)

i men ned
I wanna smell

pwehda?

i men ned

e pwoh iou
it smells yummy

e pwoh wih

I FOLLOW HER

we have to go call a taxi
the light by the store isn't working
the night is black
the moon is dark tonight
I follow her scent
she knows the way
into and over the rocks
around the betel nut and coconut palms

you just arrived from Hawai'i
and here you are walking around in the dark
she laughs currents that echo
our voices flow down the river
through the mango leaves
over to Pohn Paip and up to Pohn Pwet

I follow her short, plump figure
the glimmer of the flowers on her mwumwu
her breath
the night air, clean
when we reach the road
I look up at Saladak stars

To Swim with Eels

part of me comes from rodents
a rat surrounded by kemisik [22]
in Saladak, land of lasialap [23]
all my friends are kemisik
while I am only part kitik [24]

I could have been eaten, then
taken to the mouth of the river

the other part of me is empty
with no animals to call family
whiteness mistaken
for nothingness

I swam with lasialap girls
and their ancestors who
lurked behind rocks
and was never afraid although

I could have been eaten, then
taken to the mouth of the river

I have heard of children in Kitti
who swim with sacred eels
in freshwater pools and streams
never to be bit

my fingers bled twice from
the mouths of eels who
tried to eat the food off my fingers
a warning

I could have been eaten, then
taken to the mouth of the river

---

[22] fresh water eels
[23] the ruling clan of U, their eni (ancestral spirit) is the kemisik
[24] rat

Saladak is theirs eternally
descendents of Lien Madauleng,
their eel ancestress, who came to Pohnpei
on a school of marep
and gave birth to four eel daughters

I am not one of them
Sounpasedo, of chiefly lineage
and kemisik blood, yet
we swam and ate together like sisters
but I must remember

I could have been eaten
by kemisik girls and their mothers
long, slick bodies full,
manaman,[25]
swimming upstream
to give birth to male chiefs

---

[25] spiritual power

THE RETURN

learn how to be a lien Pohnpei[26]
a Western educated, ahpw kahs,[27]
and therefore "elite" Pohnpeian woman
get really fluent in the language like when I was nine
but this time speak like an adult
gain confidence and work experience
make some sort of contribution
write about Pohnpei from Pohnpei
maybe even learn how to make kehp tuhke and grow a pineapple
own my own home on my own land in U
go to kamadipw[28] and mehla[29]
and to Nan Dolomal and Joy
spend time with the old people
take care of my cousin and maybe some other cousins too
just be
there

---

[26] Pohnpeian woman
[27] half caste
[28] feasts
[29] funerals

THIS TIME

it was anxiety
not excitement in my stomach
I wasn't visiting
this time
a return resident
living her dream
to be on her own island
with her people
making a difference
this time
I'm alone in the sky
back at work in two days
the plane lands at Dekehtik

I feel like crying.

Pohnpei Seringiring[30]

signs of addiction
include a drying of the skin
darkening of the skin
loss of appetite
weight loss
feeling lethargic
sleeping throughout the day

sakau consumption no longer
part of tiahk en Pohnpei
except at kamadipw
when drunk out of the ngarangar[31]
in order of rank and status
now, sons and daughters
drink with their parents
once taboo
parents allow it claiming
"it's part of our culture"
"it's better than sakau en wai"[32]
even though on the inside
they know it isn't
their children sneeking off
for a bottle of Tanduay[33]

an apathy suffocates
our lush, tropical island
no one seems to care
about the landslides
killing people
sediment pouring into the ocean
choking the reefs
caused by over planting sakau for market[34]

---

[30] dry, flaky skin that results from drinking too much sakau
[31] coconut shell
[32] the sakau of foreigners; alcohol
[33] Filipino rum
[34] sakau sold for profit; also refers to sakau bars

no one can see through
the haze of
sakau followed by kapwopwo[35]
one day running in to another
by 8 pm most of the coolers
on the side of the road are empty
children wander in the darkness
while their parents drink, chew, spit
and gossip

people say
i sohte iang kang kampein[36]
kampein = free sakau
uhs ie, vote for me
but don't mention
that gas is $5 a gallon
taxis $1 in town
$2 to nan wehi
while minimum wage is only
$1.35 an hour

even a nice, cold pwotol en sakau is $3
sometimes $4

---

[35] drinking alcohol after sakau
[36] "I didn't get to eat the campaign"; politicians campaign by treating people to
sakau

THIS MORNING AT JOY

for Sipwoli

there is an African woman
eating with a white woman friend
an African American man with his
Pohnpeian sister-in-law
a Japanese man
a Filipino with his Mwoakillese wife
a Nahnep U
a candidate for Lt. Governor with
his wife and mother
a Pohnpeian businesswoman with her 3 year old son
dipping their fat pankeik into coffee
two white Americans
two ? men
all of us in this little Japanese restaurant
in Ohmine
eating

A MEAL FIT FOR A SOUPEIDI

tonite Nohno Yoko, Kadreen and I
ate makirehl mixed with karer tik and sohl [37]
mahi piaia [38] and drank upw [39]
iou douluhl,
delicious.

---

[37] Makirehl is canned mackerel, karer tik are calamansi limes, and sohl is salt.
[38] breadfruit (mahi) cooked with coconut milk (piaia) and sugar
[39] coconut

No post in colonialism at COM[40]

they say:

it's a trait *they* don't have here
they are not thorough
they can't copy a sentence
they don't eat green stuff (vegetables)
because *they* say it's pig food
it's pitiful, it's hopeless they say
they can hire some yokel dokel ding dong to do it
(on teaching developmental English courses)

it's different in the real world, they like to say

---

[40] College of Micronesia

LOKAIAHN WAI[41]

my students at COM
take ESL with me
what really should be called EFL[42]
on this island in Micronesia
Ngũgĩ Wa Thiong'o[43] would probably say
I'm a part of the colonial institution
and I'd have to agree
teaching this colonial global language
that, here in Pohnpei, I rarely even speak
except when talking to expatriates
a language my students don't really speak
their only real exposure to English being
through the TV, Akon and Britney Spears
and a little at PICS[44]

for them, English is cool
the word *Whatever!* being quite popular
sprinkled into young Pohnpeian conversations
to sound clever
an imitation of another world
full of beautiful, rich, light skinned people
far away

I attempt to use this foreign tongue
to decolonize their minds
we watch
The Land Has Eyes and *Whale Rider*
read poetry by Sia Figiel
and Mahealani Perez-Wendt
try to make a connection
across our ocean to show them
their voices and culture matter

---

[41] literally, the foreign language; English
[42] English as a Foreign Language
[43] African author of *Decolonising the Mind* who only writes in his native Gĩkũyũ
[44] Pohnpei Island Central School

I don't know if it works, but
when they see Viki[45]
chase the pigs
and her mother grate the coconut
to feed the chickens
they laugh, they identify

---

[45] The main character in *The Land Has Eyes* played by Sapeta Taito.

WRITER'S BLOCK

I'm finally sitting down to write a poem
Is it the heat?
the quiet,
not a tree stirring,
a single leaf falls from the mahi

the house darkens
the tin roof holds its breath
rain pounds the cement
and everyone in Kolonia sighs
steam rising from the pavement

what is it about this place?

SATURDAYS

I need to clean
I need to do laundry
I need to grade
I need to rest
I need to go up to U
I need to walk
I need to go to the ATM
I need to go to A-One and Palm Terrace
I need more $
I need to call my parents
I need to go to Telecom to buy a phone card
I need gas
I need cash power
I need a man

PRESSURE

Mihna needs a case of ramen for the kapasmwar[46]
Nohno Anako needs a 50 lb. bag of rice for the mehla
plus ehu kehs en malek[47]
Soulik is in the hospital again (his liver)
my cousin Reileen just had a baby
I need to bring hot dogs to the fundraiser
the car windshield is leaking
pay day isn't until Wednesday
I'm on my own

---

[46] A feast for bestowing new titles in the chiefly system.
[47] one case of chicken

ABC Ohmine[48]

we go up to U less often now
I prefer to sweat here in Ohmine
sleep under the ceiling fan in our
second floor of a house
belonging to a wealthy cousin
enclosed in the blue and white fence with hearts
always open and unlocked
with the Kosraeans downstairs
DHL in the front
surrounded by those purple flowers
papaya
a karer tree
pink bougainvillea
mahi belonging to the Mwoakillese
who once owned this lot
the leaves need to be raked up daily
then burnt, sometimes with trash

two nights ago someone threw a rock
at our door, probably a drunk
leaving an imprint in the wood and paint
we left the rock on the porch, a reminder
a fish head was once left in front of our door
our sohri have been stolen several times off the palank
we only keep the old ones outside now

in my bathroom
I listen to pakair en mehla[49] from next door
the woman from Madolenihmw singing to her children
Mwoakillese, Kosraean, Pohnpeian spoken at different times of day
UB40's "Kingston Town" played on repeat
Kadreen singing

---

[48] The lot where I lived in Ohmine.
[49] death announcements on the radio

Pwihk O [50]

I could smell it on you the first time we met
mwersuwed[51]
you were rarely home
your wife and kids on the neighbor island
a little too friendly
bragging about how you put up a light bulb
outside the house
typical government worker with a big bulge
where your stomach used to be
and black teeth, a dirty chewer
his wife must do everything
e sehse doadoak
we whispered
we had heard that about men from that island

then she came
her name meant ocean in Hawaiian
but she hadn't been swimming in a long time
she was 35, but looked 60
the children were innocent, cute

why do you do your laundry at the laundromat?
you can do it here
you insisted
in the accent from your island you told me
our machine is your machine
I would try to trust you
innocent enough sharing
a washing machine
it would save me a lot
beats 4TY [52]
$1.50 per wash and $1.75 to dry
and the driers don't even work
why not?

---

[50] literally, the pig; can refer to an animal or a person
[51] sly, dishonest
[52] popular laundromat in Kolonia

44

afterall, FSM paid for all the new appliances in your house
you would send up that special soup
people from your island make
a blend of coconut milk, fish, rice
a cooked banana on the side
delicious
I gave you fresh fish every once in a while
pilawa
let your family use my phone

I pulled up one evening
got out of my car
you were there smiling
where were you last night?
you asked
here, I said
your car wasn't here, you replied
it was in the shop, I answered
oh, I thought maybe you
spent the night somewhere
you said
as you laughed
I felt nauseous

one evening
I thought I'd throw in a load
it was just me and Nahnep
upstairs that night
I was putting my clothes into the washer
when you entered the laundry room
you asked, *where is your cousin?*
with her grandma, I said
as your wife named after the ocean came inside
so you're alone?, they asked
no, the old woman is with me, I said
oh, we thought you were alone

he said he could come stay with you
referring to her husband
and laughed her hysterical
and annoying laugh
what? I asked, speechless

he said he would come up and
spend the night with you
they both laughed, loud and frightening
he reconfirmed
yes, I told her I would come up
and stay with you

I went back to 4TY.

Ngih Kohl O [53]

for Deeleeann

I want to hide when I see that green Jeep
go by and you flash your lights at me
the way your tooth reflects sun when you smile
you think you're so hot in your security uniform
here in this small town, on this small island
where anyone is cool who has a job
or car
either can make you quite the catch
even taxi drivers think they're smooth
girls scratching each other's faces over them

please don't try to impress me
telling me about your job
those inspections you make
and your degree
how you're the first from FSM to specialize in that
you're so well traveled having been to most of the South Pacific
ooo wow
suggesting we go running
you wanna take me to dinner
I laugh and say no thank you
try to be polite
but you persist
even knocking on my door
you must think I'm playing hard to get?

oh you young generation of Micronesian men
you are so pathetic
with all your paperwork
and your government jobs
speaking English while strutting around
with that white man's attitude
your favorite word being ME

---

[53] the gold tooth

you think you're so educated
but haven't a clue about
what it means to be colonized
when was the last time you
planted something in the ground
and felt like a real man?

when was the last time you listened to the silence?

MY UROHS [54]

for Nohno

my urohs is an isimwas feast
with over a hundred urohs hanging
from the rafters of the nahs
swaying in the breeze

a kamadipw en kousapw
as women marekeiso the soupeidi
it shines on brown skin,
fragrant with coconut and seir en wai

my urohs is a lien Pohnpei
dancing and singing in a nahs in U
after winning a yam competition
the envy of the entire wehi

a seukala
for Likend
inviting her to lunch
at Joy

my urohs is a limesekedil
a weaver of kopwou and kisin pwehl
she has 13 children, 39 grandchildren
and 4 great grandchildren

a mwaramwar
of yellow seir en Pohnpei,
white sampakihda and
red hibiscus

---

[54] Urohs (Pohnpeian skirt) is the quintessential dress of Pohnpeian women, espe-
cially at events like mehla (funerals) and kamadipw (feasts). In this poem, I liken
urohs to tiahk en Pohnpei (Pohnpeian culture or custom). Urohs embody lien
Pohnpei (Pohnpeian women) and all of the things Pohnpeian women do.

my urohs is a mehla
the body covered in tehi
women with their little towels
bent over the deceased as they mwahiei

a kiam
of mahi, pwihk and kehp
taken home after a feast
to be devoured by family

my urohs is me
daughter of the lien wai
and ohl en Nan U
a iehros, walking slowly

SHE NEEDS AN UROHS

she shocks me with her beauty
when we fix our hair
in front of the mirror
her vanity worries me
she's too much like me
the boys will want to touch her
and soon she'll want to be touched
(maybe she already does)

her dihdi are no longer mosquito bites
quickly shaping into green baby mango
not ripe for picking
she's growing her hair
to be like her older cousins
with hair flowing down below their kahwe
filled with dihl and lingkarak[55]

you're gonna be different
ke pahn kanekehla
kohla sukuhl likio[56]
no babies, no boys

you know your mother lived
with us once when I was little
my parents sent her to SDA[57] with me
she was too wild
ran away and drank with boys
Pahpa cut her hair off

she likes to wear short shorts
has no one taught you how to dress?
sohte ahmw urohs?[58]

---

[55] Dihl are lice eggs and lingkarak are lice.
[56] You're going to finish / go away for school.
[57] Seventh Day Adventist School in Pohnpei
[58] Don't you have a skirt?

you need to start covering up
kowe mehn Pohnpei[59]
look at me
i ahpw kahs
but I don't parade around in shorts
like a mehn wai
and I've lived on the outside

I make sure to buy her an urohs
before I leave
she chose the red one
with sparkly cherries and
long green stems

---

[59] You're Pohnpeian.

LIKE THE ISLAND

like the island, he's always been there
and like me he grew
no longer the cute boy I teased
and called mesen kairu [60]
my secret crush

I left, he remained
when I went back for visits
I would occasionally spot him on the road,
smile and say selel
sometimes wondering
could I be happy with someone like him?
return to Pohnpei and marry someone like him
a man so comfortable
so handsome
a childhood playmate
who never left

this one time I saw him on the roadside
he had just returned from his land
shirt off, sweat shiny on his chest
like coconut oil
he was carrying a machete
and a very orange papaya
if he was a woman,
he'd have been perfect
for Gauguin
he offered me the papaya
a ripe temptation
I refused
excited and short of breath
my heart throbbed
speechless
I asked him what he'd been up to

---

[60] frog face

was he still at COM?
told him he ought to leave
and come to Hawai'i and finish
he smiled, teeth still straight and white
like when we were nine
he wishes he could
he really wants to leave, he said

the last time I visited
Nahnep told me
he was recently married
now, his wife is pregnant.

THE TREE OF INCOMPETENCE

rain for days
the huge tree fell
on October 1, 2007
behind Pohnpei State Legislature
on to the road
next to COM Pohnpei Campus
on to a blue Toyota 4Runner
on to the driver's legs
she was taken to Pohnpei State Hospital
the tree caused traffic and a power outage

the part of the tree
that lay across the road was removed
the large trunk was left
the base probably more than five feet wide
lay still
on the side of the hill
a giant's hairy arm outstretched
over the sidewalk
almost on to the street
we drive by the tree everyday
swerving over to the opposite lane
cautious it may awaken
and tip toe around it on our way
to Bank of Guam, Amcres, Namiki
we wait
for the next heavy rain
to wash the rest of it down onto the road

SEIMEK

he used to be the hardest working man in U
grew many varieties of kehp
along with uht and sakau, of course
he had many pigs
people in our kousapw called him Seimek
the fast walker
forever on his way to his land in Awak
carrying his machete
to check on his kehp,
to plant this, plant that
he'd return in the late afternoon
carrying a long pole
his prizes hanging from it for all to see

not only was Seimek pwerisek[61]
he is soupeidi
yes, he is still alive
as a child, he was adopted
by the famous Nahnmwarki[62] of U
his mother was the Nahnmwarki's sister

at first it was a slight pain in his leg
he could still go up to his land
but the pain grew
as it crept down to his right foot
the sohn wini[63] came
the sohn eliel[64] came
then he was taken to the hospital
but nothing worked
the wini en Pohnpei[65] didn't last

---

[61] hard working
[62] the paramount chief
[63] healer
[64] masseuse
[65] Pohnpeian medicine

and wini en wai [66] ran out
he had to slow down and
catch a ride to Awak
until he just couldn't anymore

he stayed home
grew a few kehp around the house
where he could
many years have passed since the days
when he was Seimek
he has risen in rank
and will soon be Nahnmwarki
still he sits at home
listening to the radio
waiting

---

[66] foreign medicine

UNTITLED

I visit him everyday
in the hospital
the pahpa kahlap [67]
I never really had
today I brought some take-out,
kahri oh idihd en uht [68]
and some leh [69]
to massage his foot
I sit on the floor, he in his wheelchair
hold his foot in my hands
my hands rubbing up from under his heel
up to his toes, neglected for so long
brown, dry flakes fall off his foot
on to my urohs
and on to the tile floor in room 208
tears for the hopelessness I feel
when we're together

---

[67] grandfather
[68] curry (kahri) and (oh) grated banana cooked with coconut milk and sugar (idihd en uht)
[69] coconut oil

ONG PAHPA

I tell him how I wish I could time travel
go back and see the world from his childhood
watch him dry copra with Nohno Lih
under the steamy sun
run across the reef with his cousin Salter
paddle the wahr with Pahpa Sou to Mwand
to pick mahi and make mahr

what did the island look like before motor boats?
I want to see Nan Peiniei
covered in long basalt rocks
that would be submerged by the tide
during weid en par [70]
their little house on stilts in the ocean
with the holes in the floor
they peeked through to watch fish swim by

the apel tree on the mountain
above the sousou, [71]
on our land
where he went to be alone

I wanna see mehn mahsoko [72]
like Lipunan, who had pelipel all over her body
and Sohn Alpet, his grandfather,
one of only three Pohnpeians to return from Rabaul [73]
i men tepweikilahs [74]
look down on the men he admired

---

[70] highest tide of the year

[71] graves

[72] people from before

[73] An island in Papua New Guinea where Pohnpeians were sent as wartime laborers by the Japanese during WWII.

[74] to look through a telescope

true ohl tohrohr [75]
pounding sakau in the nahs wearing koahl [76]

but then, I don't want to go back
like he can
and be forced to remember
what is gone

Notes

Likio

The first section of the book literally means "outside." Pohnpeians use the word likio when describing any place outside of Pohnpei. Pohnpeians in Pohnpei refer to Pohnpeians living away as living on the outside.

Sapw Sarawi

Sapw sarawi is an old saying used by Pohnpeians to describe the spiritual power of the island, which literally translates as sacred land. We believe our island is sacred given that oral histories describe Pohnpei as being created through magical power. Pohnpei actually means "upon a stone altar."

"To Swim with Eels"

This poem describes my relationship with the kousapw of Saladak in the chiefdom of U where I grew up. Most people in Saladak are Lasialap, members of the ruling clan who are descendents of kemisik, fresh water eels. Pohnpei is matrilineal and you thus earn your clan membership through your mother. Since my mother is white and my father is Pohnpeian, I don't have a clan. My father's clan, Dipwinmen, are descendents of rodents and that's why I refer to myself as part kitik, part rat.

"My Urohs"

This poem is dedicated to my mother, Kimberlee Kihleng, who conducted ethnographic research in Saladak, Pohnpei and wrote a doctoral dissertation about Pohnpeian women. Her work was my inspiration for this poem, and she continues to inspire my writing.

About the Author

Emelihter Kihleng was born on Guam, and has spent much of her life moving back and forth between her native island of Pohnpei, Hawaiʻi (Honolulu) and Guam. She has an MA in English, Creative Writing from the University of Hawaiʻi at Mānoa and spent the past year living and teaching ESL in Pohnpei, Federated States of Micronesia. She currently resides on Guam.

Printed in the USA
CPSIA information can be obtained
at www.ICGtesting.com
LVHW090258260823
756274LV00004B/386

9 780979 378836